THE NEEDLE'S EYE

SONNETS TO CRISTOS

BY

TAD CORNELL

Juggling Teacups Press

Kintnersville, PA

ISBN: 978-0-9908633-3-5 (paperback)

ISBN: 978-0-9908633-4-2 (Kindle)

Cover image from painting by Albert Bierstadt

tadcornell6331@gmail.com

tadcornell.com

Juggling Teacups Press

www.jugglingteacupspress.com

Kintnersville, PA

CONTENTS

THE NEEDLE'S EYE

From out my chest quite actual pivotal sweep,
and this man, rich in mulch, is hatching eggs
that men of science would abjure but keep
on file in case we need to change the regs.
The needle's eye is laughable to those
whose job is just to codify each chance
that foolishness might rear its head in clothes
of motley vile intention posed as stance.
Mao once payed his people for dead flies
and information on the needle's eye.
The eggs themselves have scanty chance to rise
to chief consideration, or the why
of how this camel threads himself to God.
Rich in mulch, unite! Dare to be odd!

COPY THAT

Copy that. No cyberlinks online.
But know my crew is loyal to the last.
They'll fly this crate I am despite the sign
of contradiction that has swamped my past
and from my eyes they'll melt away the scales.
Dead reckoning will be their desperate play
with camouflage of oddness, not the tales
I spin for any kind enough to hear my say.
My crew, my cloud of witnesses, my prince!
A woman clothed in sunlight, perched on moons,
is navigating all my worlds. And since
she magnifies the best of starry tunes,
we'll both be bobbing in the wake of odd.
You copy that my crew is no one's fraud?

LIMITS FRIGHT

And camouflage seems needed in this world
where axioms at "leaf" extremity
are true on grounds the axiom unfurled
from that of "trunk." Consistency as tree
will not predict geometry of wind,
much less the crazy curvatures of light.
So Euclid's truth has limits that rescind
presumptions of the past. Limits fright
is what provokes apocalyptic dread
and has us thicket bound lest birds of prey
swoop down upon our perfect pygmy bed.
The pottage at our lodge fire's thin today.
They say the simple dormouse was who dared
to free the sun from where it lay ensnared.

PALADIN

Exactly which side of that badge will you
now stand behind? No murder weapon found,
it's left to chivalry to see it through.
No easy thing to lose what we abound
in, liberty that spawns the skeptic who
in turn exterminates all liberty
with Pontius Pilate questions of the true
that alibi with shrugs the fatal tree.
The point of honor is the private room,
the ownership of property, the soul
of kings incognito, the shield from doom.
Impenitence is thriving as a goal!
O paladin to those who are unborn,
stand firm against eugenics storms and scorn.

PROPER PROPS

Events are not required to traverse
on Newton's tracks, coordinates are points
by which their motion, uniform, will curse
inertia's law while magnitude anoints.
Don't think that Galileo changes trains.
The fable of the Marshpee maiden comes
to mind. Grotesque she was, but blessed with brains
and singing voice to charm the beasts sans thumbs.
It was the chief of trouts who ran his nose
into the ground until a channel formed
from lake to where the ugly maiden goes
to sing. Their famous courtship truly warmed
the Marshpee hearts and saved their blistered crops.
Which proves events can turn with proper props.

WHOSE SURPRISE

A dandelion buckles in a twist.
The money's in the long frame played to win.
Both saints and hustlers will in fact insist
on these two truths, if with quite different spin.
Between the saint and hustler is a great
divide regarding ends but brotherhood
regarding means, persistence as the trait
they share, with focus on the ways of should.
The "dandelion" is the hustler's mark,
the "twist" the grand surprise, the tempting hope
of paradise on earth. And in the dark
they each endure for treasure's "long frame" scope.
What separates the saint from hustler here
is whose surprise is grace and whose to fear.

OUR NATURE'S CULT

There is a leap resembling faith that each
who thinks to craft a thing employs by law.
Distrust of this cognition as mind's reach
invites the justice of contempt, the claw
of snatching scavenger or pristine worm.
But here is science in its naked self,
that darling fossil never brought to term
by specialists today who keep it on their shelf
with nothing of impartial note, nor nerve
of novelty, much less tradition's soul.
But here is science as it truly is, no swerve
from real intention for transgression's role,
no certainty of foreordained result
but through glass darkly, light, our nature's cult.

UNSEEN SQUID AND SEAHORSE

An unspoilt childhood realism churns beneath
the fickle waves of adult doubts and schemes
like squid devoid of predatory teeth,
at home and glowing in our deepest dreams.
It surfaced for George Washington when he
abolished Popes Day bigotry within
his army, citing its stupidity.
It surfaced when Don John, amid the din
of battle at Lepanto, danced and sang
before he knew that victory was assured,
while back in Rome the bells of triumph rang
so sure that prayer had Europe's peace secured.
A winged horse seems natural to the man
whose unseen seahorse can inspire a plan.

Tad Cornell

DELTA FACTOR

I read about the disembodied head
of great Iamo that, alive, had teared
when Iamoqua, she who could have fled
that council lodge of enemies, appeared
and then covertly organized the plot
to rescue his mentality from grief.
The trick involves the challenge of the knot
that ties each clump of hair to false belief.
The semiotic Delta Factor in
the brain is instant, blinding in its speed,
with nothing in this lovely world but sin
to match its claim as human's radically freed.
Until some shepherds bored among their flock
were music-sent to underground and shock.

UTTER BLAME

No job for gentlemen, this training of
the troops in badlands west of Mississip.
But all it takes is evening song of love
by serenading tenors to equip
the worst of these recruits for decency.
The Mescaleros trailing to the south
have Henry Fonda pondering the three
great feints of Genghis Khan, and at the mouth
of Rio Grande he cornered old Cochise.
John Wayne is sent to parley in the midst
of hostile brave Apaches, but the peace
escapes as Henry Fonda will insist
on racist pride. So Colonel Thursday, by name,
will reap the whirlwind, earning utter blame.

WITHOUT

When music-sent, those shepherds actually found
the covert outbreak born in caves without
the celebrated sky's the limit, wound
into the bowels of earth and had to shout
within themselves how bold this quiet child.
Without is finally stamped with joy, within
quite startled into hope. If Virgil smiled
to see the mother, it could not have been
but as a shepherd with his dogs, the wise
arriving late to read what dogs will sing
upon the rising of the moon. And rise
she has, as we shall rise, from death's long fling.
But while subversion's birth is underground
the innocent are slaughtered when they're found.

THIS WINDOW

This window offers fine prospect for joy.
The handsome panorama has prevailed
with heaven's wine-stained fingers, drunk as Troy
before the ships of Agamemnon sailed.
Between ourselves and Java bones, a void
that comforts us as evening falls, a trace
of missing link, a relic twice enjoyed.
The view from here is blessed with mammoth chase.
So this is why non sequiturs are caught
among the figures painted on our walls,
or why our parables that point to Lot
avoiding backward glance, for some, appalls.
This window is the Church of Christ no less,
through which mute joy is known beyond duress.

BRAVE HECTOR

Is that our Hector? See him standing on
the walls of Priam, living heraldry.
His poise is like a metaphor gone wrong
that vindicates itself when then we see
his sword in Roland's dying hands. Poise.
The message in a bottle makes us free
where priggish knowledge yields us only noise.
And freedom is a knowing like a tree.
Oh yes, the frivolous fancies of a myth,
gratuitous as any random dream,
may seem less poised than studied science with
its simple diagrams of every theme.
But think of this brave Hector that you are
who apprehends the news of coming war.

CLUES

If we must diagram, it's you, we find,
triangulating with these words and what
they signify that constitute the mind
of Adam, you by whom the case is shut.
Consider how Red Colt, the homeless man
in Philly who dismembered his dear friend,
her street name "Angie," had the perfect plan:
to bag and hang her off the river's bend.
When caught, the well-dressed vagrant had her cash
she'd stashed away for years sewn into his clothes.
Red Colt, like Hannibal, the Grace of Trash,
had slashed and bagged while evil Moloch crows.
It's you deciphering clues from beechen grove
that wastes the dragon's Carthage treasure trove.

ANYONE WHO DARES

For one who claims reluctance to look back,
this poet's neck seems quite rotation hinged.
He's off the hook, you say, because attack
in Armageddon mode, his back all singed,
has qualified his claim of forward sight.
The context, if you will, defines the trope.
But his trajectory would then be flight
wherever history leads him into hope.
Provincial explanations tend to bore,
and worse, most often hit far from the mark.
Dismiss not those so bravely keeping score.
But know the truth is always in the dark
of forward facts inducing wide-eyed stares.
"Come forth!" resounds to anyone who dares.

MY SINUS ALLERGIES

My sinus allergies are sent by God
that I might shed more tears for loss and joy.
Remembering can be like Aaron's rod
that flowers in the private zones, a toy
within the children's box, forgetfulness
a shroud of mercy in the public square.
This body is a talking ass, much less
than Caesar's armor that proclaims beware
and more than mindless habit can confess.
But then the dying leaves or sprouting seeds
will mount the breath of life as if to bless
my labyrinthine membranes with His deeds.
As tears erupt, rejection of the Man
by men collides where only memory can.

KONG

The panic that ensues when Kong explodes,
defying interlopers to his shores
where he is jungle king, in fact corrodes
my trust in valor by conquistadors.
For them it was the black swan that we dread.
It came from nowhere, bigger than the best,
survivors just amazed that they aren't dead.
For Kong it's all routine. He beats his chest
more often than a Muslim prays, his life
a constant slaughter of the dinasaurs
who populate his land, Fay Wray, his wife,
unlikely to persuade against such wars.
If only Kong, when captured, understood
that art can conquer everything for good.

A SEARCH

A search for the black box is underway.
It lies somewhere inverted in the pit
of Java seas, like "stomach" in the play
we term morality. Medieval wit
and Dante call it Hell. The ribcage trunk
is Purgatory's shape, quite upside down.
Our only hope is pilgrim's feet, not sunk
but water walking, deadly errors found.
Our Paradise portrays the human head
that reads the vestiges of this great loss.
"Levati su . . . in piede!" So we're led
by Virgil's intuition of The Cross.
Commenced the climb to beatific bliss
where Gloriana's face is not amiss.

THE AFRICAN QUEEN

So Katherine Hepburn and her brother pray
when hearing of impending war from him
whose stomach gurgles: Bogart. This screenplay
was filmed in Africa. And Bogart, limb
from limb, is slowly reconstructed by
the lady in the river's seaward path.
The crocodiles and Germans dearly try
dispatching Rose and Charlie in the bath.
The insect plagues of Egypt are among
the trials their growing love will have to face.
And just when legend's valor, song unsung,
is doomed to vanish with no human trace,
the Barque itself, dismissed by demon horde,
dispatches them, prayer answered by the Lord.

MR. SOFT TOUCH

Glenn Ford and Evelyn Keyes are bumping heads.
The smell of poverty unites them here.
He's called Joe Miracle, and she, with beds
for orphans, Jenny Jones, endures the fear
that Joe, a common thief, cannot resist
possession of his only landslide score.
The story ends with tragedy's worst twist,
a miracle that dies at nothing's door.
What isn't told by film, I here relate:
Our Joe becomes the Osage founding snail
in Purgatory's world, in death's late state,
Great Spirit feeding him that he might scale
to snail-man glory in the Osage tribe.
Just so, the fate of poets may subscribe.

ENDLESS TRUE

Apocalyptic rhetoric, the art
of essay composition for the stew
that stirred the Spartan will to stand apart
into the gospel of the endless true
produced the founding of the Stars and Stripes.
The essay genius is the sonnet's charm,
with Genesis trajectory for the types
of Patmos vision, vials of wrath and harm,
that we, benighted readers, might repent.
The sermon of John Witherspoon, his name
just signed on treason's desperate document,
proclaimed that law must clothe man's hapless shame.
Who knew the essay form endorsed by time
could prove itself the art of sonnet rhyme?

STARING UP A CLIFF

Or is it more like chess? Duchamp renounced
the royal crown of peeping Toms for chess.
The pieces were just garden sprites that flounced
within a geometric rule unless
the pauper peeper took the champion's path.
I do not know what path he took, or if
that game became for him his heart's own math.
For me, it's more like staring up a cliff
where brigands hail down missiles toward my head.
Our siege machine is climbing up the ramp
and soon our enemies will all be dead.
Tonight I'll sleep in this Tenth Legion's camp.
I'm just a soldier sent to do a job
though once I was more like a regal slob.

MUSIC IS THE SYSTEM

The clouds of sophistry accumulate.
It takes the judo of inversion in
this world to see the strangeness that our fate
has brought us to, quite sleepless in our skin,
a kind of cripple wrapped in fashion's best
and shaken with the madness known as mirth.
In this, and more, apostles stand the test
that sophists fail who, like the simple worth
of beasts, could never try to hide their root.
That unknown god, that missing link, is seed
among the dung, he says, which they find cute
that he should be the bird of Word indeed.
But broadcast live, when asked the message sent,
"Music is the system," spoke young gent.

PRESERVING VIRTUE

Preserving virtue was the project of
the New World colonies that broke from kings.
A *tabula* quite *rasa* was the love
that to this day is ringing, eagle wings
of new life imitating natural law
and stamping into governance the just.
"Send not the rich away" begins to knaw,
Charles William's tale of Arthur's holy trust
in Bread that's broken over earthly Grail.
And music truly is the system here.
It's mediated by Our Lady without fail
in keeping virtue, banishing all fear
in this, my land, as taught on father's knee
about the brave whom legend calls the free.

NEWNESS PRIZED

Reductio ad absurdum proves the new
that hackneyed observation will dismiss.
So don that mortarboard hat and gown of true
academy and try imbibing this:
Nine months from when Tom Jefferson swore-in
as US president, on New Year's Day,
John Leland, Baptist clergyman, who'd been
that atheist's partisan along with they
in Cheshire, Massachusetts, gave a gift,
a mammoth block of cheese, to Jefferson.
"Obedience to God," their motto's drift
across that cheese, "is tyranny undone."
Which goes to show the mousetrap best devised
will bait with aged stink for a newness prized.

RING OF BRASS

To catch the ring of brass requires time,
not effort quantity, but time itself
as friend, a gift of gab, a gift of rhyme
that spellbinds time. And charmed like Tolkien elf,
beyond old Einstein's wildest dreams, time's stopped
in lion tracks at words here spoken now.
Those words allow the ring cannot be dropped
because our jailor, time, declares just how
its strength is in its maker. History?
A precious gift in light of Light Just Said.
So how is time cajoled? I just can't see
how nuptial promises and holy bread
transform that beast to circus mastery!
You've put your finger on the mystery.

FINGER ON THE MYSTERY

Success, brass ring, is shaped for hands
to execute grand glyphs so broadly short.
The carousel implied is shifting sands
we funnel for our progeny's report.
And circles? Just a mercy, second chances,
repetition meant to keep things straight.
And built to last, with passing nature's dances,
chimes a second mercy, precious freight
like gold in how ennobled we'd become
if loving life could win us one step more.
Don't let your finger stray, or get struck dumb.
We're drilling down into the cosmic core!
The lion and the lamb together, bold
and real, for you, at will to then unfold!

LIGHT JUST SAID

Light Just Said can penetrate disease.
It banishes a demon at a twist.
It answers calumny alone to please
the will of Light, Who, with tears or holy fist,
has guaranteed the software true to Life.
It breeds the rivers rushing torrents through
to blighted lands and souls. There is no strife
that Light cannot illuminate and do
what's needed here and now. Just Said, it was,
Whose footprints stir the faithless in their sleep,
is making book that you love words because
you love to dive for pearls into the deep.
At each day's snatching for the ring, we plod
on ground we're best advised to tread unshod.

EXTINGUISHING IS . . .

"Extinguishing's the devil's favorite game."
More than game, the stakes so high that lore
of mythic charm could gladly murder same.
Poor Sorrowful Jones returns, bound to adore
through cautionary tales, old myth so new,
to offer training tips to neutralize
the threat without incurring sin, the true
and beautiful an object truly prized.
The seminar was canceled. Wintry mix
was all it took to silence Mr. Jones.
The devil's lust for death does take its licks
with every consecration, Cross in zones,
the art of fishing with our God as bait,
our hook, and arm that lifts the evil freight.

HOUTHI SPOOKED

His memo had us truly Houthi spooked.
The fate of Yemen hangs on if that tribe
will join Iran to see the Jews all nuked.
Old Sorrowful is not your standard scribe.
His messages are posted on the web
in cryptic fashion, always on the run,
and no one ever thought him a celeb.
But be advised, it can't be too much fun
for his deep throat to wander desert sands
like some Beau Gest with feathered secret sign
for "this just in," as unseen offstage hands
here shatter our fourth wall before we dine.
"The Houthi who inherit this grand coup
bear watching like a wooden horse and crew."

.

THE MEMO

The memo that most irritated me
from Mr. Jones was, "Don't forget to shovel
hydrants," like a snow alert will see
our risks controlled endorsing public grovel
before municipal authority.
There's barely mention of the global scene!
His reportage is only geared to we
who trust self-interest as the nation's theme
as constant Protestants for virtue dreamed.
For him tradition must erupt in bursts
while fault-line data dictates what is schemed.
He makes no room for sacramental thirsts.
We rarely see him kneeling at a shrine
or celebrating feasts with holy wine.

IMPUNITY?

He'd like to think he's Hector in a suit
for divers in the old-time films they drop
into the pitiless deep, as if the loot
below could plant a kind of Rome, and stop
the pain that mythic contest here exacts.
He weds himself, like Bonaparte, appeals
to history, his only god, and acts
as if impunity here dogs his heels.
The Fool is freely dealt for such as he.
My patience tested, conscience in exam,
I fall asleep and saw the cherry tree
that George confessed to kill the sham.
My Sorrowful Jones, you're welcome after all.
The water hydrants must indeed stand tall.

Tad Cornell

GEORGE WASHINGTON

George Washington is apt as case in point:
A man becomes an instrument of global good
by self-design, but bowed for the anoint
of Providence on human grounds of "should."
A Protestant perfected, or at least
quite shed of all but selfless Christian will.
He's ever wary of the foreign beast.
Divided government, no random pill
dispensed without prescription, quite intent
that lust for power has sufficient leash.
For this he gave his life, a man quite sent
to send the preachers out to really preach.
And justice is the nation's jubilee
where virtue thrives like blossoms on a tree.

COVERT MISSIONS

And then it strikes me that the Navy Seal
just interviewed is Jones' prototype,
and to a tee, the humble warrior, real
in every way. In boyhood, fully ripe,
he dreamed he could become protector of
the innocent whatever race or creed.
You'll never see him duck, but up above
the camera shows him ducking in the lead.
Dishonor's risk more dreadful than one's death
unites us with antiquity if Christ
had never come. He says it in one breath.
His covert missions spell the perfect *geist*.
The face we see on every dollar bill
is righteousness at odds with evil will.

THE CORPUSCLES

The corpuscles of human life comprise
a universe designed of dazzling things.
It's well to pause and reassess if lies
have any place in medicine. White wings.
They flash in old-time camera starlet style,
a blinding grand proposal with the banns
no less than chiseled into winsome smile.
This body's truce, in kicking down the cans,
with body language spoken with a thrust
while babbling with its itchy stinking urge,
is comedy about a gangster's trust
in his dear trophy gangster's moll. The surge
is impotence of tyranny in face
of enemies that vanish without trace.

JOHN LOCKE

Physician to Lord Cooper, one John Locke
would rise to philosophic fame in face
of atheistic monad trends, to rock
the world with claims creation's binding case
must hence cement man's claim for equal rights.
That royal beast we mostly know as time
became what liberty from royalty here cites.
Its beasthood recognized alone is prime
in claiming, without dogmas, God supreme.
This New World principle, where many come
as one in liberty, was more than dream.
It was, and is, a fashioning, a drum
that beats the cadence of the faithful dead.
Its sum is more than parts awkwardly said.

MANABOZHO

So if, indeed, this grand created world
is property of Him who fashioned same,
the right of property is here unfurled.
The case against King George would then inflame
a parliament that only Edmund Burke
would vigorously argue to the sane.
A legend, Manabozho, seems to lurk,
who lost his son to evil spirits' brain.
A voice, in all his grief, sent him to where
such spirits congregate, and there disguised
himself as a humble stump that wouldn't care
if they should desolate the land he prized.
For him, it took a handful of this earth
to give that land its very worthy birth.

IN DISGUISE

The Catholic world is featured in disguise
where this great birth occurred in history.
Elizabethan stark jihad did rise
to equal Roman cleansing of the plea
of Incarnation, curse of Christ. The state
defends itself like white cells in the blood.
Extermination failed. But don't inflate
the seeming random data turned to mud.
The blood of martyrs never sheds for naught.
The Protestants who mostly made this birth
of nation overseas had never sought
conformity to any worldly dearth
of Gospel claims. Madame Curie, you know,
Greer Garson, basks in radium's subtle glow.

THE *TILMA'S* SHAPE

Yes, to our southern neighbors she'd arrived
long since in all her glory that is stark
with miracle and humble cast, survived
of Aztec and conquistador brute mark,
where native seers confirmed the message sent
designed into the *tilma* of her shape.
The pregnant maiden seems to be intent
on winning souls by torrents. Even rape
can be survived in hidden holy light.
Not hidden like the pagans, secret wiles
reserved for the elite, but private sight
endowed with freedom despite trials.
Her basking in the rays of what is new
survives the test of natural as true.

THIS JONES OF MINE

Old Sorrowful is tapping out Morse code.
He thinks my broom is sweeping much too wide.
Too wide of what? Too wide of wisdom's road?
Too wide for anarchists to finally hide?
He's marketing personified, where in the field
the thing that counts is brand that closes deals.
Strategically, his plans have no appeal
beyond the stubbornness he clearly feels.
The global view requires pondering.
And then decisive acts. A policy
toward Houthies need not rhapsodize and sing,
but should be of one cloth, not stop and flee.
This Jones of mine I love, and love to hate,
thinks all will come to those who simply wait.

NEVER REALLY TAUGHT

Who knew those gospels, four, would be enshrined
forever such that ignorance of such
deserves derision everywhere? To find
a place among the doctors that's no crutch,
like deconstruction's suspect nonsense ploys,
is clearly where the seeker wants to be.
From there one's mind is made by honest joys
of reading them for what the mind can't see.
On titan shoulders everyone must stand.
Enough, these slanderings and obtuse slights.
They've had their day, the avant garde their brand.
Quite unassailed, they reign today by rights
they captured like some hostage ISIS caught.
They claim a Koran never really taught.

POSTSTRUCTURALISTS

Poststructuralists assemble on the quad
to stop the Catholic poet in his tracks.
Religion has no academic place on sod
prepared for mental tombs and student snacks,
unless its tribal lore, Islam, or Jain,
Vedanta Hindu, Buddhist, or the Tao.
It seems that only we espouse the rain
that falls on all, from bleachers plow
the seed of life transcendent into art.
It seems this "Incarnation thing" stands out.
It threatens sophists most, who actually start
assuming art is never nature but about
an arbitrary construct fixed in space
by chewing gum and random abstract lace.

HANDS NOT CURSED

When nature equals jungle, sophists thrive
with every other predator that prowls
the halls of government. Those who dive
for pearls of wisdom line their Darwin bowels.
So you demand this poet legislate,
with Shelly's will to purge our inward sight's
familiar fog, reforms that just can't wait?
Here Mr. Jones is tweeting Goethe's lights,
how boldness furthers providential growth.
And there it is, the alternate law, a world
that starts repealing all that tempts our sloth,
and nurtures with organic plan unfurled
to grope for best together, creatures first,
but inward bound to build with hands not cursed.

THOSE GOSPELS

Those gospels, though, won't feed and house our broods.
They are no blueprint for our uncursed hands,
nor Gilbert's "cataracts of platitudes"
to which each moralist subscribes and stands.
The Man who walks these pages is quite more,
or other than, what should comprise a creed.
The absences, hesitations, the scenes that soar
transposing humble coin to bondage freed . . .
Astonishment at every turn, a part
where every character will seem to breathe
their passion as libretto breaks the heart,
more like an opera than how religions wreathe. . .
His time had not yet come, he said at first,
his quest now launched to end in desperate thirst.

ANTHEM SECURITY BREACH

Identity is compromised, it's true.
A thief or blackmail monger can obtain
whatever feeds its caliphate, and you,
your narrative, starts dribbling down the drain.
First to go, they say, is anthems in the soul.
But this occurred before the solemn breach
that waits for all who live so long. It's droll
as prostate destiny for men, but reach
into your narrative for what won't swell,
dismiss, or die without an anthem sung.
And purge it of the heretics who dwell
in Mithra's bull or empire's Arian dung.
The anthem that provides security
defies all uncreation with a key.

HIJACK EXPERT

It came as shock to learn that Sorrowful Jones
was Anthony "gas pipe" Casso's firstborn son.
Old Tony, Jr. turned with righteous groans
against that legendary mobster, won
a life vendetta free, no longer split
between one's reason and one's cultic acts
that makes morality the bitch of spit.
The Man the gospels show presents odd facts
of something in the life of this "Gas Pipe":
an expert in the art of hijack at
an early age, all business, coming ripe
in bypass plundering of banks. I sat
with gospel pearl in mind, that industry
as great as this for Him would set us free.

PLANT THE COMMON PIETIES

If I don't plant the common pieties,
with all the diligence a witchdoctor ploys
to hatch his miracles, where I can seize
when my dementia leaves me only toys,
I'll forfeit knowing Him for far too long.
The still waters He's led me to have teamed
with life, and You are with me, like a song
that lures me to all corners of what seemed
extremity, riding thought itself
almost like He does, not just naming things
but making things that fly from off the shelf
as introduction to the You that sings.
What joy! But be advised you're not too good
to wear His priestly vestments like you should.

THE BLUE DAHLIA

So, "Once you've found her never let her go . . ."
Not only does she wear as glorified
those vestments, she is making them quite so
as to enhance your ever striving stride.
The woman, like Veronica Lake for Ladd,
will intercede. You know this from the start
no matter how you try to pose as sad
that she is queen of all that could be art.
Alan Ladd eventually gets the point.
Sincerity. However masked by slime
of devils at Blue Dahlia, it's a joint
that never touches her, a fact in time
unraveling in a weaving sort of way
that promises that she is here to stay.

YOUR HEARTFELT SONG

But first of all, she's antidote to this
pernicious Desert Father's fight with thought
they named *acedia*, the bane of bliss,
a fungus as it creeps, when all that's taught
is not enough to even bury the dead.
These thoughts can make the petals on the wet
black bough of Pound a thing of silent dread.
The apparition of those faces set
within a crowd assumes a dreary cast
as planted bombs tick down to doom's effect.
But she defuses fungoid thoughts. At last,
the struggling hermit's soul cannot be wrecked
because she mediates those graces on
the execution of your heartfelt song.

BUT MR. JONES

But Mr. Jones has got some trenchant points.
Precision is invention's final test
regardless how necessity anoints.
Defeating torpor also means the best
of strategies employed, the most
inclusion of the birth, and Day of Rest.
And this just in from Jones: This evening's host
now broadcasts from his Desert Father's chest
the lub-dub proof his domicile's a cave.
Expounding Guido Cavalcanti at
the Eiffel Tower, troubadours the rave,
he'd flown into my room, a frantic bat.
Precision is finesse in nailing things
that move like targets borne on angel wings.

THINGS POLYPHONIC

He'd crashed their party, back before the war,
in London of the dueling manifestos.
Direct treatment of "the thing" was something more
than cabinet maker's chitchat as the shops close.
It was a mystic creed between H.D.
and Aldington. Discussing it brought strength
to hone the revelations (with an earnest plea)
erecting wet, black boughs of various length
for city halls. They honed toward classic lilt.
And Amy Lowell, Madam *Kairos* herself,
was overflowing chalice till it spilt.
(If I'd been there.) Jones, the one whose shelf
has wealth of memories, seems somehow bereft.
Things polyphonic dawn like happy theft.

A QUEST

I, of course, am holding out for grand
revival of Pre-Raphaelite works. I'll call
it Post-Raphaelite. Original as sand.
For me "the image," yes of course, is all,
that quiet complex piercing with no sign
to warn us, only gasp. Oh yes. But when
does more than spareness not come here and dine?
When does quest turn guns of treatment again
toward everything? But on, direct to Thing!
The only thing worth knowing seems so strange.
It's the only thing worth having. Here's a ring.
Humble gift, Post-Raphaelite flourish, arrange
the furniture as you like. It's not abstract.
It's Thing Kong top of Empire State, last act.

ORBITS

You'd like to volunteer to go to Mars.
They're planning the first launching as we speak.
While shuffling up in basements, future scars
announced themselves inheriting the meek.
But Mars for life, a colonist on land
as bleak as mind allows, is lunacy.
Two moons are really more than you can stand.
Already preparation is the key
that rules the day and night. So why rely
for breath on constant wild consistency?
You posit home as no more orbits, try
to see yourself as Martians need to see.
But orbits are the floor show booked for here,
this anywhere you go, this world so dear.

INHERITING THE MEEK

Now innocence insatiable will blow
its frigid wind through every window crack.
It's filled with seeds that only mean to grow,
all scattered in the snow. It won't take back
its gusto for the failure of our grid.
Inheriting the meek is power's job,
its heaven-sent vocation and its bid
for statues someday toppled by the mob.
A purpose in the bowels of things will spread
in most destructive storms. Earth's Sacrament
has landed in this Rock, transformed from bread.
But all too few, the planters that are sent
when spring renews the compact of the meek
and lifts its scars that innocence we keep.

THE TRIAL

The trial of Gilbert's Mr. Innocent Smith
made history: cross-examination banned
for witnesses but hailed for lawyers with
each other. Justice misses what seems canned!
If truth were really what the law would find . . .
And Gilbert stresses that such testimony
should be "vicariously" induced to bind
opponent counsel, homicide or alimony.
And it proceeded Perry Mason style,
the center of the earth arrived at, more
dead center than our Wells, and all the while
a research into what is truly core.
It turns out seeing double is the trick
for any jurisprudence never picked.

PUDDLES

The vindication prayed for wends its way
in tumbling second thoughts toward sea,
in sleepy ponderings for brighter day.
The puddles on the way to Mass would be
our Gilbert's warning of how cruel the stars
are known to be in academic cant.
The "ugly secret" pythons souls in bars
where man-boy students still enjoy a rant.
His grand declension of the German flaw,
confusion of the will to live with joy,
from High Dutch to that Double Dutch. We saw
how declination angles death for Troy.
A brighter day may have to wait for Rome
where founding history finds its natural home.

ETERNITY

Eternity's the idol we erect
to rival God, dear Gilbert simply said,
the dream of, lost in space, the grand prospect
of being found deferred. I'd put to bed
the triumph of all science as a cause.
I'd say forgetting also serves when slaves
are bred for service not of natural laws.
I'd say that reason dictates what he craves,
an innocence that leaps and hangs reversed,
a human Tarot card, the Hanged Man,
that thwarts eternal worship of the cursed.
The ecstasy of separation can
be, has been, known: the things of art.
But mythos is just cud without the heart.

NOT A JOKE

Old Sorrowful is claiming that he knows
what Gilbert means by "heart." His message comes
amid reports of that Black Hole that grows
titanically from that first instant, glows
like no hole ever could. Not sentiment.
Or if it were, the longing it implies
looks more like solidarity that's bent
on loving truth and killing aimless lies.
The aiming does require mystery,
or metaphysics bravely played for keeps.
Impossible as that Black Hole we see
in space. Yet real. Or so his memo leaps
into the fray avenging exile's stroke
with merriment that proves it's not a joke.

THE GLUE

Here, breaking news. Her mediation of
these graces is the thing of utter pause,
that substance of the crazy thing called love.
The pause of wonder is the best of laws.
Her antidote to dismal is that step
that locates where you are and wonders why,
and then remembers why like God's own rep.
Your calendar is dismal purged. You try
to stay here where the tents for Moses and
Elijah would have been, and only she
directs your gaze between the two, her hand
directing orchestras of one by three.
The concert that she engineers is true,
which means that holy silence is the glue.

THE STREETCAR

The streetcar that brought us here is coming back.
Of this there is a certainty beyond
what stellar divination yields to crack
what Stanley meant by waving cupid's wand,
Napoleonic code: take interest in
your wife's affairs. Sweet Blanche is shining jewel
of Old South lion taming, leads by chin,
a charm informed by history's tragic school.
She's opposite her sister's passion. Which
is best for policies toward brutal men,
those "every man a king" types, and women bitches?
Refinement is endangered species! Can
containment policy of vulgar Pole
succeed? See modern hero, perfect role.

INTO THE SEINE

And Jones himself had shrieked poor Stella's name
with equal pain, been on the lam since then.
Like undercover journalist, he came
to London's Eiffel group, the golden pen.
His cover name was Fletcher, born and raised
in Arkansas, where cornered flees from corn.
But now he's either dead, his work ill praised,
impersonated by some actor's horn,
or recluse hermit finally free of these:
the difference it would make with different warts
and pride of fly balls that a man can seize.
We just don't know the source of his reports.
The street car has long since arrived again.
Inspectors throw themselves into the Seine.

FOUR WALLS

He once espoused the theory that a man
must learn to stare at doors, imagining
that people come to visit. Then he can
compile the witness grand surprise can bring.
Just why compiling things deserves to rise
to place of honor never was quite clear.
Directness was the rage back then. The size
of compilation had no weight. You steer
instead with reckless conjuring of apt.
They say acedian devils had him pinned
like anthill feast, still dreaming he's all wrapped,
a specimen that never really sinned.
His theory is debated in the halls
of hermit's minds who dare to test four walls.

FREEZER PACKAGING

He actually froze some vital parts of him
like freezer packaging, which may account
for why the tundra seemed much more than whim
for such as he who dreads a thaw. Amount,
he said, can play no part erecting what
survival must demand of organ pipes
that toot in concert, dark as pipes are shut.
A high note hit by frozen part then wipes
the chalk board clean, he said, the only way
to multitask the soul toward certain war.
The operation faces cancer today.
His plan is telecast, a plea for more
of everything that kills this enemy
who froze the part that makes the conscience free.

PAUPPUKKEEWIS

Reminding me of Pauppukkeewis, he
was aimless in a search for random thrills.
He hid from death by species change, a tree
an otter, beaver, bear and elk he wills
by special powers to become. He reigns
as tyrant in each of his adopted homes
and suffers painful death, never refrains
from bad decisions, his spirit ever roams.
It took the hero Manabozho to
at last make terminal that power spree.
Or so they say. His lightning species true
had struck where human hid inside a tree,
and finally perished Pauppukkeewis here
where hiding is a last resort in fear.

COCOON

He died so many times disguised as tree
or otter, beaver, bear and elk, and rose
from each the human that he was, to free
his spirit from tradition's cocoon that froze
the will, he said, for change. Now Gilbert leans
into this tale. Cocoons can incubate
for life unseen, of human spirit's scenes
that all are pointing up and never late,
invited guests to banquet with the Lord.
Sorrowful Jones can hear the plaintive tune.
See him long for Manabozho's sword,
repentance ridden, grief revealed as boon.
Just so is sacramental grace bestowed,
a prince from what was once an ugly toad.

BOGGY OCEAN

We must begin with boggy ocean, what
our microscopes see daily just to know
that death lurks not in what we drink. But,
first glimpse of the first bog! We'd have to crow
and take it Glasgow-way. They have to see.
The evidence is documented here.
The chicken soup at first dismissed as plea
is plea indeed. Her intercessory tear
can pierce the night with mother's panicked cry.
Dogs begin to howl, and birds take wing.
This ocean bog's alleged too big to die,
it gears itself for one more time to sing.
So, sixty-six is one for every year.
The bog I've met is I, the stakes quite clear.

THE ANGEL

The angel who brought distance to the bog
was Manabozho. Clarity was snapped,
with focus then the challenge, braving fog
to lead a people who will not be trapped.
So next, we need to study this great gift.
You find it in great statesmen: happy space
whose time has come, pause, the very rift
that shapes a thing or stirs a fervent chase.
In just this spirit, wiser men than I
have mounted hurricanes of virtue to
bombard the gates of heaven, and then try
dismissing honors earned in being true.
This gift appeared in ocean bog, they say,
the space between, perspective's royal play.

DANTE'S ARROW

Examine Durst, among the worst in crime.
A billionaire whose murders are bizarre,
his eyes so dead no everlasting time
is long enough to light on who we are.
Perspective was the first he jettisoned.
Pride was mainlined, taunting the police,
the needle's eye the gate he always shunned,
a mumbled mutter that can never cease.
This vivisection must be faced by us
who see these traits contaminating life.
There is no exit, nor a magic bus.
Durst's choices are the origin of strife.
And choice is more than matching consequence,
it's Dante's arrow, blessed common sense.

MOTHER'S PLEA

They knew it in Kentucky. Methodists preached
what now is called Awakening, Part Two,
in this the land of Manabozho, unimpeached.
They preached tent meetings vast and true
that swept the nation. Thousands agonized
each night repenting sin. These rallies, odd,
instead of altar calls had featured, prized
by Catholics most, the Supper of our God.
Our Uncle Gilbert would remind us, if
he could, how Mother's plea was unseen key
to graceful oil for necks Kentucky stiff.
He'd vote the Manabozho ticket, free
and clear of homicidal suicide
that preys upon the virtue of The Bride.

EQUINOX

Migrating flocks will learn to recognize
their landmarks on the way, distance won
in high style, squawking signals always rise
and fall. They risk the bog and hunter's gun
to meet the planet's deadline, equinox.
This day the moon is biggest in the sky.
Just so is heaven's kingdom filled with rocks
that hurdle through with scarce a reason why
until theology has made its case
for seeming random threat for every sigh.
Thus Uncle Gilbert spoke, without a trace
of evidence he said it, as per Jones.
Could be the universe is passing stones.

Tad Cornell

STURDY WALL

On this same day eclipse obscured the sun,
was seen by fools and wise men, west to east.
The judgment comes when no one dares to run.
Instead, the next Barabbas is released.
Again some Greeks ask Philip for the Lord
and voice in thunder marks a crumbling world.
See how we love one another, speak in accord,
never shirk a chance for flags unfurled.
Unwinding every length of shroud as I
have here, we closely trace the rise and fall
in eons of past empires asking why.
The scholars have a job like papal call.
They're nailed here upside-down, forgiving all,
and building facts into a sturdy wall.

PROCEED

Our nation's sins we see too well, quite schooled
are we in how our cotton industry
that put us on the global map had fueled
the slavery evil in the land of the free.
Or Georgia's wars with the Creeks, disgraceful fleecing
of a people. The gift of distance fails us when
our telescope turns in. Laments unceasing
never heard from souls could deafen men.
We need a second gift to land among
our spires like leaflets, marching orders, hope
that corners will be turned and goodness sung.
But sin can fool you with its rope-a-dope.
"The gift has come as promised," leaflets read.
"Anoint your doorpost, then in faith proceed."

PIVOTAL SWEEP

Quite actual pivotal sweep occurs unbidden
and secret hatching poised to swarm the earth
will prove why eggs are always first kept hidden.
The egg is not the end-all or the birth
of progress, Gilbert says, "efficiency"
its only claim to fame. Toward what, you ask?
Unbidden, but comprising human we
who hatch into this world with awesome task,
the bird, ideal Platonic, predates egg.
Its life is source and final actual end,
the only insight questions do not beg,
the remedy a mother's love would send.
The eggs I hatch are not what I can keep.
I celebrate each actual pivotal sweep.

A TREAT

Reduce it all to looking homeward and
you find, stampeding elsewhere, futurists
with fashion-hungry gaping mouths, with sand
where anthem pours foundations and resists.
Elites of every stripe behave the same
and always have, as any cowboy knows,
predictable when spooked by any lame
decree of skepticism, promptly goes
to sleep when any threat to homeland's real.
Ideal of home they deem as ruined dreams.
They're doomed to novelty, the endless wheel.
All vision stops at only how sight seems.
Predictable and dangerous, things effete
are trampling out our vintage like a treat.

BOLD PROMISES

And Sorrowful Jones had fallen prey to this
stampede toward what is not by what is new,
his vines in shreds by hooves of specialists.
Discouragement became the only true,
authentic stance he had to meet the world.
A suicidal pilot locks out home
from Jones' cockpit, flight plan madly hurled,
bold promises that he would no more roam.
Or is he lab rat sent to orbit earth,
a man whose mission creep would almost mock
our father Abraham whose nation's birth
was son here offered on Moriah's rock?
This home, so simple, still defies a quip
or exposé, so subtle: State of Ship.

EQUAL UNDER MISSION

A density beyond analysis
is man's mundane domestic rituals,
as Gilbert says, all democratic bliss
achieved in taverns with grand victuals.
Equal under mission has no rules
that anthropologists can catalogue,
those simple things, like how a soldier fools
himself he's dead already, hugs the fog,
when facing bullets. Rules like these are known
by tales of burning bush at second rounds
of beer beside a burning log. I've shown
how things unsaid by futurists abounds,
discouraged as they are by history's plight.
Their victim, home, won't quit without a fight.

MY DEFINITIONS

My definitions, far from being meant
as creed persuasion, are but arrowed broad,
heraldic license, diagrams FAX-sent
with reasons to see threat and what to laud.
We start from dawning vague enough to start,
assignments given, roles are taken, faith
the student's champion and very heart.
Our hands are branded by a wandering wraith
who claims us with its vicious fleur-de-lis.
Lesson one, forget those pendulums
they teach, where bodies swing for all to see.
Across the land I hear the angels' drums.
Beyond a wall, a childlike voice now speaks,
"Take up and read," strong words for one who seeks.

THE GREAT MAN VOTES

John Barrymore, who drank a quart a chance,
was victim of the grand works of the party,
down and out, disgraced. That Gregory Vance
should fall so far! The Childrens League, quite hardy,
found his empty bottles. Now they'll take his
children. Girl and boy of once-great Vance
are loyal to delusion, though smart as he is.
They bargain so the ward boss risks his pants.
He makes Vance education's commissar.
Vance now leads the grand parade to the polls.
He wins, of course, the girl, who's shown so far
will see promotion to his staffing rolls.
His speech to multitudes is unsurpassed.
Her "perspicuity" recognized will last.

EDUCATION

So education, Gilbert says, is not
a "thing" with features like a woven rug.
What violence is its actual ontic dot
that threads the needle's eye, or quells a shrug
and bargains for his father, Gregory Vance.
Alleged to live in temples that will need
a commissar to feed it in some trance,
real education pierces like a seed.
It parasites the core of our free will.
The arbitrary SIM card wreckage found
has video, horrendous panic, still
someone was teaching straight into the ground.
And ever learning, we will take that ride
from sky to earth till error cannot hide.

MORTIFICATION GOLD

A corner's turned when physical exercise
is mortification gold. Decline has reared
its head and shakes with dubious warning cries.
I'll have to trust my cradle skills. As feared,
this learning curve reduction spells my end.
Here mother's care returns and ceiling cracks,
are faces, cobweb mobiles drift and bend.
The nurse is revelation, heaven's tracks
that range my skin with commerce firm in mind,
strategic promise where no nothing lacks.
The miracle is she, so hard to find.
The gold is hidden in all life's attacks.
The rivalry that education schemes
goes on between our birth and addled dreams.

GOOD CONFESSION

That being so, and time so very short,
confessing how I'm slave to peeve and sloth
I hope will be the Gordian slice retort
that ends with legend's holy flame to moth.
It's what comes into us, not prodded out,
that makes for good confession, earnest plea
for help, sincerity beyond the doubt
so both illuminate the tomb to be.
But short cuts aren't sincere, unless they're true
discoveries, since the prodding can't help see
or asses the swill of all things fashion new.
So feed the lambs who stray just to be free.
Pegasus, descendent of that colt
Christ needed, tours me, candor's flashing bolt.

EGO

Among my crosses, and it never ends,
is suffering fools who claim the ego stalks
our mental health. Such grip on modern trends,
affixing to poor ego's rap sheet "walks
the dark side," proves the fools thus suffered are
the fools they seem. Jihad deflating each
of us before each game would only scar
a good man's name. That simple. Then I reach
into the splintered wood they leave behind
and start to reconstruct the crime scene, sharp
as some Aquinas, one would hope, but find
I'm just an ox who learned to play the harp.
My wanted poster is my claim to fame.
But what I want is ending this damned frame.

THE PERFECT CRIME

I'm sounding like my friend old Sorrowful Jones.
Please let me take the podium one more time.
I sense approaching dawn, my teacher's bones
are churning marrow. Here, the perfect crime:
the truth. No violation else can ever make
the headlines, "Social Justice Now Assured."
Truth telling is the art we've lost, the fake
and faint of heart have means to have you lured
into a harem-heaven where your ribs
are gone, your lungs and heart exposed, one cured
of everything but using soap and chronic fibs.
Our survey says that only truth has toured
those old crowned heads, though here disguised as meat
for student bones when taking to their feet.

SINKING TRENDS

If Madame Kairos were to now descend
in *deus-ex-machina* style, she'd read to us
of legends told among the tribes of men.
A case in point, it's Wassamo whose fuss
spread wild across Lake Michigan. It ends
with Wassamo and his spirit wife who wade
into the lake, waving, sinking trends,
when piercing wail as red flame feather blade
went glancing on the billows, image seized.
The tale begins in a classic fishing trip,
with Wassamo and unnamed cousin pleased
with giant catch. But Underworld's dark ship
had snatched our Wassamo as cousin slept,
and cousin faced a murder charge and wept.

HUMAN COST

Now cousin was left holding gossip's bag.

While Wassamo toured Sand Mountain with his bride,

his cousin languished, hoisting desperate flag.

Redemption day occurred in time, the tide

was turned with Wassamo's return to earth.

The spirit guardian of Nagow Wudjoo

is actually who arranges things, from birth

of romance for his daughter to the true

and pentecostal ending, flaming tongues.

But what about that "let them eat grass" crowd

that pilloried cousin! Have we lost our lungs?

Sans evidence or motive, or a loud

and winning lawyer, cousin nearly lost

his life. The message is the human cost.

GENDER FED

Yes she, almost the Queen of Angels, read
this story to my class. And bedtime tales
forbidden for a woman, gender fed,
erupts as controversy in the sales
of video scandal, she, the renegade
from feminista dogma hereby nailed.
Like cousin on the rails, her lawyer played
the "indefinable forces" defense and sailed
her client into gender jubilee
when my summation flew into their ears.
I quoted Gilbert: ". . . new as an idolatry,"
but nothing new in rank ideas, these fears
a woman's famous memory wins the toss
and man's world suffers futuristic loss.

LASTING MELD

The need for bedtime stories seems to sneak
into this lecture. Madame Kairos shows
from her whole history, climbing to the peak
revealed as cherished anarchy, that so goes
those things immutable that reason dies
to seize which get dismissed by civic plan.
Why? She battles vulgar blatant lies!
But "what is truth?" is asked across the land.
It looks like Martha Washington who held
Mount Vernon while her husband took command
has more to say about the lasting meld.
The hearth she cultivates is concrete's sand.
If civic fervor were my call in life,
I'd think a statesman needs a holy wife.

MOTHER DRAGON

Her "old man" George, she realized when she met
his evil-tempered mother in his bleak homestead of
Ferry Farm, what scars must yet
attend him. He formed himself to always seek
and warmly give the good, the true, the fine.
For him, Mount Vernon is a miracle
of desperate jail break from ancestral mine
to found a life. A home. Empirical
grand anarchy ideal baptized in love.
She came to know and do a sacred task
that binds us to a final Noah's dove,
the home no government can justly ask
its suicide for common good. To think,
this George had plans to sail the seven seas
when Mother Dragon beat him to his knees.

INTENTIONAL

So Martha Washington, known as Patsy, met
her massacre at Monogahela when
her little Patsy died. In this, a net
had snared her, dragged her to the pen
where grief torments all mothers' fervent souls
who lose the light in their sweet baby's eyes.
Like him, with bullet holes through cloth, no holes
through mortal flesh, they faced two mothers' lies,
two wars for independency. A birth
as raw corporeal as any spawning
labored into a world of law and mirth
was engineered, a nationhood's rare dawning.
An art is that which must be personal
but may be quite perverse, intentional.

THUS GILBERT SNEAKS

Thus Gilbert sneaks in there the final drive.
What would he make of the 1960's show
on my TV of "Wanted: Dead or Alive"
with Steve McQueen? As Josh, the slow
to win at cards but fast to slap down clowns,
is chasing Martin Landau, Khorba, who
stampedes his elephant through frontier towns
to rob the fleeing populace, the new
and thrilling Glory Brothers Circus parks
outside of Tombstone. Medea herself invites
him in to lounge, and not that there aren't sparks,
but Josh has seen the elephant and fights
his inclination to comply. Three times
he asks himself why he must solve these crimes.

TRUST

A threat across the Rockies sweeps the floor.
It's more than little Hannibals that must be stopped,
or even crimes that all would plain abhor.
It's why we need to have this class, we've shopped
enough for angles, ism's, gizmos. What's plain
is what to trust. And trust for what is key.
The threat begins on science fiction's train,
a raising up of insects where we see
like congregants who kneel to twisting pall.
Legends like our Jones, at least he knew
the worst, that microbes found in space are all
we'll find of life, no insect pal and true.
The rich in mulch will have to hold the floor.
The game is on, so Katy bar the door.

FAST EXPLAINED

Consider washing, whether clothes or self.
Its mundane process somehow quite unites
in pause, the future folded on a shelf.
St. Joseph Cupertino's frequent flights
impress one less than Trinity explained
by folding cloth. The pause for silence kept.
In washing, dignity is never drained.
Your failures rise as noble prayers. You slept
through pity for yourself, then providence
was raining doves into your furrowed brows,
your knowing that a clean defining fence
you trust for home is worthy of your vows.
How simple are the things that truly last.
Such things can redefine what's meant by fast.

CONSIDER UNION

Consider union, man and woman, "birth,"
as Dr. Zorba on "Ben Casey" chalked
on blackboard, "death," a cross, of worth
in signs of science, then a final talked
through flourish, sideways eight, "infinity."
Solemn theme song then commenced, with cheers
in every throat of we, watching TV,
who need a cause that compensates for tears.
Who doesn't? Man and woman form the beast
of burden that is meant for babies blest,
but not for those who only most as least,
the last as first, though each aspires for best.
The best, my friend, you know as well as I
is sideways eights with nature's earnest try.

WITHOUT A SCORE

The Book of Matthew starts with lineage
that proves the Son of David walks among
us, kingdom of beatitudes is pledged.
You'll know him by the washing sung,
the weddings, and now healing oils as well.
Tell them that demoniacs are freed
and paralytics walk, hemorrhages quell
and parables bring dignity to seed.
Anointing that should follow washing is
the seal of heraldry that binds a son
or daughter to King David's bright show biz.
Only bounders would refuse that fun.
But what I've outlined isolates the core
of what unites us all without a score.

CHIVALRY IS CLUE

The household's head brings from his storeroom new
and old. Anointing of the sick shines well,
and chrism that is chivalry is clue
to what is closest to the war with hell
that no one living would not die to fight
if called like Simon, son of Jonah, to
the task, the prayer unceasing, facing blight.
These are yearnings deep and humanly true.
The counterfeits exploit this basic need
recruiting terrorists. A hero's born
each moment. Evil's ever strangling weed
has nothing new in perverse love of scorn.
The rosary is actually Christ's own way
to victory in Lepantos of today.

CONSOLED

Analysis of flight disasters haunts
the reason for this class. They offer tips
on what the errors likely are, and wants
us comprehending lift dynamics, ships
that shorten space itself, possessed of speed.
Decisions in the cockpit wrestle time.
It's obvious enough, but no less what is creed,
what doctrine is, what prohibits the crime
of sloppy thinking or the loss of nerve.
The need for critical thinking came with death,
and taxes close behind. The fruit deserved
is targets planned, a pilot's skills, and breath
of life redeemed, and then forgiving sin
as due ordained, consoled and gliding in.

RED APPLE

Red Apple hanging low from Christian root
was coveted by Byzantium's sultan lord,
and nothing less than conquering and loot
of Rome was his by raising his crescent sword.
The last of Europe's noble knights, Don John,
was summoned by just second of holy popes
in quite some time, a modern trend, a dawn
for the Church with Europe on corruption's ropes.
The victory at Lepanto Don John led,
that Pius V had seen by vision, changed
the course of history. Rosary prayer had fed
the fiber of that army otherwise estranged.
All this to show how thinking critically
is best when knowing whence comes true mercy.

THE BRIDE

The Bride condemned for "prime directive" flaw
is criticized when she cannot do more
to interfere with Earth's own Bernard Shaw
much less each psycho killer's ugly score.
Has she denied our world is drunk by flood?
Has she made claim to anything not sealed
in promises Christ signed in His own blood?
That this should all be sensible, appealed
to by just reason, yes it can by natural law.
But only Word Made Flesh would really do.
Sensible. Surprise that bends, nets draw
to what is nature, captain's humble crew.
Upon this rock a Solomon some scorn
will guide the Bride in mending what is torn.

Tad Cornell

MINDLESS BLIGHTS

If interfering were the primal slight,
the raisin farmers would not have to sue
the government for unfair regs that bite.
And governments will hold a gun on you.
They'd have us red-tape garlanded and broke,
a prostrate slave to bureaucratic whim.
Since Church proclaims that seed is not a joke
and pertinent to civil life, hope's dim
that Caesar won't announce another purge.
The seed they shun is sacred washing, oil
that heals, the oil that seals (Lepanto surge),
the pledge of man and woman, honest toil
in planting absolution, and then lights,
two more, that root against all mindless blights.

WAS WHAT BID

Fornicator bandit Anthony Quinn
comes riding down the aisle as Mass concludes,
and passes out, the soldiers riding in
pursuit. Old Fr. Joseph then intrudes
with claim of sanctuary, smuggles him out,
but dies in San Sebastian. Quinn can't shake
the peasant faith in him as priest. He'd shout,
"I'm no priest!" Exasperated, he'd take
to chiding them for bellyaches about
how Yaquis and then bandits raid their corn.
"Defend yourself, you cowards, see you pout!"
They all cleared out. But this was normal, torn
and tattered peasants, they, who lived and hid
out in the woods. The church bell was what bid.

Tad Cornell

GUNS OF SAN SEBASTIAN

They all came back, processed through town joy filled.

They'd heard the Father's sermon. They would fight.

Here St. Sebastian is carried, arrow quilled.

Dismayed, Anthony Quinn was caught by right

of ownership to pose as priest for his flock.

He came to see the habit as great disguise

and lobbied for his village. What a shock

when Father, with troop escort, then supplies

the rifles, ammo, even cannon . . . one.

They build an almost castle-formidable wall.

And something changes in our priestly son

of old Fr. Joseph's death. He now hears the call.

The trust but verify approach to him

has grown in every single shepherd's limb.

MY CITING MYTHS

My citing myths is not at history's cost.
The gnostic heretics attacked the thought
of Son of David history. These lost
in wonderland say making myth one aught
to call last word in truth. If that were true,
as poet, mobs should herald me as king!
No justice could be trusted. Who to sue?
No, this is error. Let me simply ring
the San Sebastian bell and chant the prayers,
and underscore how Christ was like a sperm
that pierced and fertilized our history's cares.
Our myths are happy whimsy. What is firm
is Uncaused Cause alive in time, new speed
for bandits who can try not bruise the reed.

WAKE US

You'll notice the grand arrow in our thought
on history since that date of pregnant dawn.
St. Matthew's sweeping portrait has us caught
in saving nets that never fail, from drawn
depictions of a kingdom come to last
commands for His submitted witnesses.
Centennial of Armenian genocide is cast
as first such evil in our modern bliss.
The story should be Komitas, the priest
who salvaged from those ruins his nation's songs.
The Hubble eye so humble is the least
of precious witness of where our trust belongs.
The piercing of our hearts by history's lance
can sharpen minds and wake us from our trance.

COME HOME TO GROUND

My old friend Jones is texting a retort.
He says the priests of cycles, pagans, yes,
have long since won the mob's trust in the court
of Xerxes for the verdicts that address
a future that must lay its past to rest.
This genocidal rulership of mind
exterminates its failures with its best.
It claims a virgin birth by man's design.
But Simon Magus tried that silly bribe
for powers that claimed thrust, and Mecca bound.
Madame Kairos said once to that tribe
to stop their piracy, come home to ground.
It's envy born of fear that stalks their souls.
Their management of terror heaps their coals.

DISCIPLESHIP

Discipleship, submission to the best,
remains the leading motivation here,
in this same world that crimes abound like jest.
The crony-capital predators don't fear
discovery when discipleship is banned.
But best is crucial target for the knight
whose drive has languished, nicely tanned,
in dissipated compromise called flight.
No legislature bent on squandering search
for what is best, convinced of tinkering crude,
(that bread and circus spasm with a lurch),
will have the wits to duck when votes intrude.
The best is staring like a mother in your face.
So little knight, go forth, redeem the race.

BREAD AND WINE

You have the best that reason has yet found.
You have free will. You have a world. You see
with inner eyes the plight of all. Would sound
of Word Made Flesh be any less than we?
That sound could consecrate the water, oils,
the breath of vows and mercy, and it does
if one allows that changing "could," that boils
the egg, to "should," that peels the shell, it was
His favorite hard-wire cog in our poor mind.
No sweat for AM WHO AM, transforming things.
Which brings us to His crowning bread and wine.
For this the bell of liberty here rings,
and all across our world wherever hope
is given its full consequence and scope.

BY THE SHORES OF GITCHIGUMA

Consider Pauppukkeewis, known for tricks,
a "harum scarum" fellow by the shores
of Gitchiguma, in the famine, who picks
his way to icy pinnacles where roars
the spirits who inhabit there. He begged
them for relief. They told him, fill your sack
with ice and snow and don't get pegged
by looking back at shouts behind your back.
They said at a certain hill to stop and leave
the sack just overnight. He did as told,
and morning's sack was full of fish. Believe
me, word got out. So Manabozho, bold,
made that same trip. But angry shouts of "Thief"
and "Take away" seduced his own belief.

WORK THE PLAN

And how could source and substance, simple, take
the shape of so much complex plot where death
itself is secret victim, life for life's sake
indeed risen, cast of thousands blending breath?
This God could only be a kind of Shakespeare.
Who knew this grand and simple story's just
begun? The mercy was we're made to hear
simplicity of tone and screen-out dust
and fury. And yet climax in The Cross
is all. Catharsis is a balm, like holy oil,
simplicity restored in knowing loss.
And yet entwined is more to know by toil
and all the other dignities He wants for man.
His own, alive and dead, now work the plan.

Tad Cornell

CANTICLE

But *eschaton* aside, the mystery of mulch
persists. And eggs are what it's all about.
I'd have to save the lady at the gulch
like any other self respecting burnout.
(They pay money for scripts like this.)
Those things entwined I might yet know,
like waltzing, the harmonica, stoned bliss,
the party that old Sorrowful would throw.
It's here where bread and wine belongs,
a send-off through a needle's eye, count down
for miracle that stalks with cadenced songs.
The feast on Him He gives us is His crown.
The wine and bread is more than meets the eye,
and more than sweetest canticle good-bye.

ABOUT THE AUTHOR

American poet and performer Tad Cornell (T. H. Cornell) was essentially an underground poet after his first book, *Glance Over at These Creatures*, was published in 1977. Some of his poetry was distributed conventionally, but more was personally bound and hand-gifted, presented in poetry slams and avant garde stage productions (in Hong Kong, Houston, and Philadelphia), and on guitar and vocals as part of poetry fusion rock band, Edgar Allen and the Poettes, and other ensembles.

Cornell's s childhood until age twelve was in Germany where his father worked for the US State Department (as a CIA agent, Cornell later learned). He was a child opera star at the Frankfurt Playhouse, and studied theater and wrote music in high school in suburban Philadelphia. During three semesters at Goddard College, he was inspired to pursue poetry by Paul Nelson. Cornell earned a BA in English from Temple University, a master's degree in special education from Antioch College, and a master's degree in English literature from Villanova University. The special needs of his only child, born with spina bifida, led him to a thirty-year career in social work. At intervals along the way, he was drawn to consider the priesthood, served as a Trappist novice in the Abbey of the Genesee, and studied theology in Rome at the Angelicum.

Other work by Tad Cornell

Blue Heron Rising (Juggling Teacups Press, 2015)

In Whom Is My Delight (Juggling Teacups Press, 2015)

The Unspeakable Mating (Latitudes Press, 1989)

Honey From the Rock & Hong Kong Elegies (Latitudes Press, 1988)

Glance Over at These Creatures (RHD, 1977)

CHAPBOOKS
The Graphics of the Mouth (2006)

Gloria Über Alles with Stan Heleva (script and score, 1999)

It Seems Important (1988)

The Promise of Silence (1978)

Rosie Knuckles Knows (1978)

Cough Poems for the Tickle (1978)

Looking the Moon in the Face (1977)

Hollywood Diamond Exchange (1977)

Marco Polo (1977)

www.ingramcontent.com/pod-product-compliance
Lightning Source LLC
LaVergne TN
LVHW021522080426
835509LV00018B/2607